Samuel Egerton Brydges

Verses on the Late Unanimous Resolutions to Support the Constitution

To which are Added Some Other Poems

Samuel Egerton Brydges

Verses on the Late Unanimous Resolutions to Support the Constitution
To which are Added Some Other Poems

ISBN/EAN: 9783337157708

Printed in Europe, USA, Canada, Australia, Japan

Cover: Foto ©Thomas Meinert / pixelio.de

More available books at **www.hansebooks.com**

VERSES

ON THE LATE

UNANIMOUS RESOLUTIONS

TO SUPPORT THE

CONSTITUTION.

TO WHICH ARE ADDED

SOME OTHER POEMS.

By SAMUEL EGERTON BRYDGES, of DENTON, in KENT, Efq.

CANTERBURY:

PRINTED BY SIMMONS, KIRKBY, AND JONES:

MDCCXCIV.

ADVERTISEMENT.

THE following Trifles have lain neglected, and almost forgotten for some months in the warehouse of the Printer. When almost finished at the press, they were somewhat prematurely announced to the Public; and an accident then prevented their publication. But in consequence of that advertisement, it becomes at length necessary to submit them to the inspection at least of the few friends and neighbours for whom they were intended. The first poem was hastily written at a great political crisis, December 19, 1792, *and sent immediately to the Kentish Gazette, in which it was then inserted. The rest are* mere trifles indeed, *most of them written at least ten years ago, and of their fate the author is entirely careless.*

DENTON, *Jan.* 9, 1794.

VERSES,

ON THE LATE

UNANIMOUS RESOLUTIONS

TO SUPPORT THE

*CONSTITUTION.**

HARK! 'tis the shout of joy that meets my ear;
And Concord's plaudits shake the echoing sphere!
" Long live our glorious KING!" And long may live
The blessed days that Law and Order give!
And may our children's children still enjoy
The sacred fence, that villains would destroy;
And ages hence in peace and plenty smile
Beneath the shelter of the noble pile!
Mark how Sedition's clam'rous tongue is drown'd!
Mark how his looks his frustrate schemes confound!
Mark how the guilty Plunderer scowls to find
His golden visions vanish'd like the wind!
Mark how the Murderer grins, since now no more
He hopes to wash his savage hands in gore!

* Written Dec. 19, 1792.

And Envy foul, and disappointed Pride
In sullen gloom their dreams would vainly hide
O'er their Lords' necks with cruel taunts to ride!
O hail to Britons' generous hearts! that brave
All storms, the cause of Liberty to save;
But, still to Wisdom and to Order true,
Licence and Anarchy with hate pursue!
O meliorated scheme, that Time has drawn
From many a struggle past, and peril gone;
From Wisdom acting on the deeds enroll'd
Of many a wond'rous Sage, and Warrior bold!
O Constitution, with more power endued
To curb the Vicious and protect the Good,
Than e'er the page of Hist'ry told before!
And shall we prize your happiness no more?—
O civil Policy, whose power prescribes
Riches and safety to Barbarian tribes;
That from the woods the houseless wanderer calls,
To the sweet shelter of surrounding walls;
From where, o'er scanty and uncertain food,
Naked and shivering half their hours they brood;

Or o'er drear wilds throughout the tedious day
With endless-toil pursue the needful prey;
To the warm vestment; to the chearful dome,
Where sure of safety each commands his home;
Where still the bread, that wholesome Toil may get,
In peace his little tribe may round him eat!
O Policy! not only such thy praise!
Mankind to higher bliss thou yet can'st raise!
To touch the heart, to feed th' etherial flame,
That seeks by polish'd arts immortal fame;
Manners to soften, soothe the maddening strife,
And teach the sweet civilities of life,
'Tis thine, blest Power!—And thine to scatter round
The useful splendor, with which Wealth is crown'd!
Hence Labor finds employ; the Poor are fed;
The industrious Artist's board's with plenty spread;
Hence Commerce lifts her sails; and hence explores
The world's wide circuit for its varied stores!
Guarded by thee, sweet Policy, by thee!
The fruits that, borne o'er many a dangerous sea,
Months of sad peril and long toil employ'd,
In peace securely are at home enjoy'd; Guarded

Guarded by thee, the Swain who tills the ground,
In safety sees his harvest ripen round;
Nor o'er the spoils of savage clans he weeps,
But the same seed he sows, himself he reaps!
Guard as thou art then, guarded may'st thou be
By future ages resolute as we!
May Justice wave her sword, if Faction rise,
And stop th' audacious Coward's treacherous lies!
Woe be the day, that sees the Villain lead
Destruction's hell-hounds to the rueful deed,
When all that's fair, and all that's wise, must fall,
And Waste and Desolation cover all!
Ne'er may I see the hour!—but should my doom
Lengthen my life till such a conflict come,
May the first sword be pointed at my breast,
And in the quiet grave secure my rest!

VERSES upon ANCIENT MANSIONS.*

HAIL, ye bold turrets, and thou reverend Pile,
That ſeem in Age's hoary vest to ſmile!
Thou noble Arch, thro' which the massy gate
Opes to yon Hall in slow and ſolemn state,
All-hail! For here creative Fancy reads
Of ages past the long-forgotten deeds;
Tales wrote in magic marks thy walls among,
By Time's ſwift current as it pass'd along.
Hail, virtuous race! Whoſe Sires from age to age,
The gay and grave, the Soldier and the Sage,
Here, where you still in happy peace abide,
Caught their first breath, and here in quiet died!
Yes here the bold Cruſader from his toils
Return'd t' enjoy his long-lost children's ſmiles:

* These were written for a friend, as part of the Preface of the 2d vol. of the *Topographer*, and were accordingly published in that work.

Yon

Yon pictur'd window, where the doubtful light
Bursting thro' mellow panes enchants the sight,
Rais'd by his hand with Glory's honest flame,
Shews the bold Cross the emblem of his fame;
That Crofs which still with spirit undecay'd
Against the cruel Spaniard was display'd,
When *Raleigh* led his bands from shore to shore
New worlds with dauntless courage to explore.
Yon old hereditary trees that spread
Their rude luxuriant umbrage o'er your head,
Their grateful shade, two hundred summers past,
O'er the soft slumbers of your Fathers cast!
O ye wild dells, ye hills with beeches crown'd,
Ye opening lawns, that yonder pales surround;
Within whose circuit, still alarm'd with fear,
At every quivering leaf-fall, leaps the deer;
And unrestrain'd by modern bounds, to find
His ancient ranges shoots before the wind!
Ne'er may the Stranger, rais'd by lawless gain,
Disturb the peaceful Lords of your domain,
Pollute these haunts by cruel rapine won,
And ope your hallow'd umbrage to the Sun!

But

But the same race, that blew the bugle horn
Along these echoing woods to cheer the morn,
When the fourth Harry heard the lively call,
And grac'd your lord in yonder feastful Hall,
May the same virtuous race your echoes court,
Pursuing still th' hereditary sport,
And roam in summer suns, or rest, beneath
Your lovely shades, and catch your fragrant breath;
And, still in death the same desires to keep,
In yon low chapel with their fathers sleep!

SONNET.

WRITTEN AT WOOTTON IN KENT.

WHILE I re-wander o'er this wood crown'd steep,
Yon sheep-clad lawn, and this secluded dell,
Yon Mansion, and yon holy Tower, that peep
From the thick trees, where in their silent cell
The hallow'd relics of my fathers sleep,
I strive in vain the tumults to repell
That force mine eyes with sad regret to weep,
Since my sweet childhood's lost delights they tell.
Here my lov'd PARENT pass'd his happy days
In rural peace, with every Virtue warm'd,
While the wide country round, that rung his praise,
His sense directed, and his goodness charm'd:
But I, alas, to genuine pleasures blind,
Tost on the world's wide waves, no quiet find!

SONNET.

On MOOR-PARK, *near* FARNHAM, SURRY, *formerly the Seat of* Sir WM. TEMPLE, *whose heart was buried in the Garden there.*

To yonder narrow vale, whose high-slop'd sides
Are hung with airy Oaks, and umbrage deep,
Where thro' thick shades the lulling waters creep,
And no vile noise the musing mind derides,
But Silence with calm Solitude abides,
TEMPLE with joy retir'd that he might keep
A course of quiet days, and nightly sleep
Beneath the covering wings of heavenly guides,
Virtue and Peace.—Here he in sweet repose
Sigh'd his last breath.—Here SWIFT in youth reclin'd
Pass'd his smooth days! O had he longer chose
Retreats so pure, perchance his nicer mind,
(That the World's wildering follies, and its woes
To Madness shook,) had ne'er with sorrows pin'd!

SONNET.

THE WINDS.

Aug. 23, 1784.

SUBLIME the pleasure, meditating song,
Lull'd by the piping of the winds to lie,
While ever and anon collecting, fly
The choir still swelling as they haste along,
And shake with full Æolian notes the sky:
A pause ensues; the Sprites, that lead the throng,
Recall their force, and first begin to sigh,
Then howls the gathering stream the rocking domes among.
Methinks I hear the shrieking Spirits oft
Groan in the blast, and flying tempests lead,
While some aërial beings sighing soft
Round once-lov'd Maids their guardian wishes plead:
Spirits of Torment shrilly speak aloft,
And warn the wretch, who rolls in guilt, to heed.

SONNET.

TO THE

REV. COOPER WILLIAMS, A. M.

FRIEND of my early childhood, since the wane
Of the declining year no more invites
To bask abroad in air, while falling rain
And the cold blast the wand'ring footstep frights
From miry-pathways, and from field-delights;
In this old mansion, where the pictur'd pane
With pomp of ages past enchants our sights,
Here let the blazing hearth our hours detain!
Round the glad board while wine, inspiring wine,
Liberal not lavish, aids the' unbending mind,
Let my wild gloomy fancy, joy divine
In the mix'd sunshine of thy humour find!
For worldly storms, and every eddying blast
But bid us to old friendships cling more fast.

SONNET.

AN EVENING IN MAY.

YE glittering Stars of Heav'n's blue concave, Hail!
Ye ancient Oaks, that lift your branches high
In the dim twilight of the azure sky,
Beneath whose arms I hear the Nightingale
Pour out her liquid notes across the Vale;
While mates from every half-leaf'd covert nigh
In exquisitely varied notes reply!
Thou faded hill, where bleating Lambs bewail
Their mothers lost! thou hedge, yet dimly seen
That skirt'st the Meadow, whence the shcreel-owl cries!
Ye glancing lights, that oft by fits, between
The opening branches, from the village rise!
Hail, soul-composing scenes, and harmonies,
That raise the soul to heavenly extacies!

SONNET.

OCTOBER.

October 13, 1784.

O LOV'D October ! still my vacant day
 As thou return'st, in rural sweets shall fly !
 Mid yellow fields ; mid woods of tawny dye,
 Whose fragant leaves about my pathway play ;
By russet hedges ; all thy morns I'll stray :
 And round the chearful fire in converse high
 With choicest spirits meet, when o'er the sky
 Soft social Evening draws her mantle grey.
Nor will we cease, till Midnight's reign profound,
 The sweet communion of the fleeting hour,
 While blasts that yet but weakly whistle round,
Urge to enjoy the moment in our power,
 Warning of winter-days in tumult drown'd,
 Far from the quiet of the rural bower.

SONNET.

No more by cold Philosophy confin'd ;
By fearful models now no more deprest ;
I give full range to my erratic mind,
And with wild visions soothe my beating breast !
Hail, thou lov'd season, when the hollow wind
Strips the torn forest of its golden vest ;
Shrieks in the echoing domes, and frights the hind,
Who sees sad spirits thro' his broken rest !
But while the rain descends, and while the storm
Bursts in loud eddies thro' the sobbing grove,
Spirits before my view of heavenly form,
And scenes of wond'rous beauty seem to rise !
Sweet Inspiration's voice my Fancy hears ;
And verse immortal seems to meet my ears !

SONNET.

AH me! vain wish! the vision cannot last;
  And sad reality must undeceive!
  The painted shapes of Fiction's loom are past;
  And Truth's dull hues with keener sadness grieve.
Yet shall the Muse a grace, tho' mournful, cast
  O'er the deep sighs she taught the breast to heave;
  Shall turn to music every wailing blast;
  And light with fairy rays the darksome eve.
Weary of Hope; by cold Neglect subdued,
  No more tho' Fancy imp her eagle plumes,
Yet shall she soothe the melancholy mood
  And throw a smile on Disappointment's glooms!
    Soft are the woes, with which the lyric string,
    Unheard by mortals, makes the forest ring.

SONNET.

Supposed to be written by WOODVILLE, *at his Castle of* GRAFTON.

From the STORY of MARY DE-CLIFFORD.

YE mould'ring towers, these waters deep surround,
That, age succeeding age, the forest-shades
Of yon romantic wilds have proudly crown'd!
The voice of Revelry no more invades
Your dreary courts; nor yet with tuneful sound
Do royal Edwards* woo the Aonian maids
To melt the Fair, who on their suit have frown'd:
But, shook by Time and Fate, your glory fades.
No more shall Beauty with her winning eyes,
Brighten your halls, and o'er your feasts preside;
But sad and lonely, while your master flies
O'er foreign lands his sorrows to divide;
Silence shall reign along your chearless walls,
Save when disturb'd by nightly spirits' calls.

* Alluding to Edward the Fourth's courtship of Elizabeth Woodville, at that place.

Description of ELLEN St. AUBYN.

FROM AN UNFINISHED STORY.*

IN Truth, she was a wondrous beauteous dame,
As e'er was sounded by the trump of Fame!
Slight was her form, and tall; her taper waist
Was short; its circuit small a girdle grac'd;
And from her milkwhite garment's wavy flow,
Her slender ancle sweetly shone below:
White her plump hands, and soft round-rising arms,
Whose blue meandring veins encreas'd their charms;
But more her opening bosom caught the sight;
Firmly it swell'd, and beam'd forth rapt delight;
As polish'd marble smooth; as driven snow 'twas white:
And most the blooming beauties of her face,
Her cheek's soft roses, and her forehead's grace;
(This white as lilies; those of livelier hue
Shone fresh as in the fields, when dipt in dew;)

* Written in 1784.

Her ivory teeth ; and chief, her soften'd eyes,
Like Cynthia's beams, which gently light the skies,
With more than mortal bliss the gazer fill'd ;
While her light auburn locks, that sweets distill'd,
Around her neck, and cheeks, and forehead play'd
Luxuriant, and diffus'd a varied shade,
Whose tints divine no painter e'er essay'd !

E L E G Y.

Written in November 1782. *To Mrs.* LEFROY, of ASH, *in* HAMPSHIRE.

ERE yet in Cam's dull walks and croaking school,
She faint beneath cold Reason's chill embrace,
My Fancy pants one favoring hour to rule,
And weave a wreath my sister's hair to grace.

Sweet nightingale, since I like thee with song,
While others slumber, sooth the night away,
Oh! give thy power to lead the heart along,
Thro' the soft thrillings of the plaintive lay!

Then as I bid the fairy fabric rise,
Of prattling Infancy again to view,
My melting voice from every list'ner's eyes,
Shall call forth pensive Memory's pearly dew.

For well, my Sister, claim thofe boyish days,
The foftest strain my feeble powers can give,

And well dost thou deserve my warmest lays,
If any lay of mine may hope to live.

'Twas then, if ever in this world of woes
She deign'd to reſt, that bliss indeed was mine,
And then, if ever in my breast it rose,
To light the flame of rapturous thought was thine!

Ere yet my infant feet had strength to stay,
Dryads and Wood-nymphs caught me in their arms;
With them explor'd I every cave by day,
And all their wildest haunts, ſecure from harms,

By glimmering twilight, list'ning to thy tale
Of ghosts and goblins round the hearth we hung,
And thought we heard their voice in every gale,
And started as the Fays the death-bell rung.

With some strange story constant as the night,
By thy lov'd voice my frame to sleep was laid,
When mimic Fancy roſe at Reaſon's flight,
And with redoubled force each ſcene display'd.

But when thy footsteps led me to the Fane,
Mid thickest woods embower'd from vulgar eyes;

(Where

(Where as they watch'd in dell and narrow lane,
From their green beds the peeping Nymphs would rise,)

That Fane where Poesy, resistless dame,
In melting state has plac'd her rosy throne,
My' enchanted soul quick caught th' ætherial flame,
And vow'd eternal love to her alone.

Blest be the hour, beyond all others blest,
That saw me captive in the fair one's arms,
And ev'ry blessing crown my sister's breast,
Who taught my youth to prize her lasting charms!

EPISTLE.

EPISTLE.

To a Friend, *on a Visit in* Lincolnshire, *August* 9, 1784.

ON THE PLEASURES OF VICISSITUDE.*

****** ! My Muse, to thee, whom most I prize,
At Friendship's altar lights her sacrifice.
Thou dear companion of my early days,
To thee from childhood was I wont to raise
My voice, and fear thy blame, and love thy generous praise!
Tho' harshneſs in my rugged lines displease,
Yet mellowing Time shall make them flow with ease;
For when the Fancy's flame, and force of thought,
A deeper energy of soul have wrought,
Then varied like my mind shall pour along
The strong, yet tuneful current of my song.
But now when manhood ſcarce has strung my nerves,
When every power too oft to Pleasure swerves;

* This Poem is an attempt to imitate the freedom, variety, and energy of Dryden's *Rhythm*.

How

How shall I tell thee all I think and feel ?——
E'en now I see thee from the circle steal,
In some lone spot to feed thy restless soul,
That scorns by vulgar barriers all controul ;
And longs to fly to other worlds, and bursts beyond the goal.
But mortal powers, for flights ſo daring weak,
Must soon descend, and humbler pleasures seek.
Some beauteous maiden now, (for Beauty e'er
Twin'd with my thoughts, in all will have its share,)
I see thee tending ; in her converse sweet,
For wearied powers to find a soft retreat.
With the smooth cheek to feast the raptur'd sight,
To watch the beaming eyes with fond delight ;
Be sometimes yours, and sometimes be it mine !
For that dear pleasure, I can ne'er resign.
Vicissitude, oh lov'd Vicissitude,
Thou bring'st the soul with zest for joy endu'd ;
Thou giv'st the rapture to the lonely hour,
And to the social, thou its kindling power !
E'en now from thought intent, and inward light,
As bursts on yonder yellow fields my sight,
With double joy the golden scenes delight :

The influence thine, more fresh the scenes arise;
Inſpiring Autumn, with her gleaming skies,
And all her merry harvest-train, comes dancing to my eyes.
And now perchance, as Fancy points, my friend,
While his slow steps thro' evening homeward bend,
From gothic castles, and majestic walls,
From gloomy gateways, and from ecchoing halls;
Spies some warm cot, and owns thy influence there!
What double raptures in his eyes appear,
To find Content, and Peace, and Mirth within
Thoſe little walls, so low, so weak, and thin!

Yes, lov'd Vicissitude, and e'er may he
His taste for pleasure quicken'd find by thee!
From social intercourse, and social good,
Seek the pure pleasures of the lonely wood;
Thence plum'd his feathers, fly again to man,
By practice strengthning what his thought began!
In constant pleasure if desire we steep,
The palled powers in dull stagnation sleep:
E'en the dear idol, for whose fancied joys
We'd lose the world, in full possession cloys!

May I, [nor ſmile, my friend, thro' varying ſchemes
Of life with me are fickle as my dreams,]
May I, in life ſome gently active part,
Enough the joys to heighten of my heart,
Chooſe—Whether steering in the toils of Law,
Or wishing silent Senate's ears to draw.
Whate'er my fate; in bliss, or in distress,
If power adorn me, or if want depress;
Thee ſtill my friend, [may heav'n but grant me thee
Thro' Life!] my anchor shall I find to be.
May I, thro' many a year's improving round,
Whatever fortune shall thy wishes bound,
As firm, and faithful still to thee be found!
Adieu! may Beauty's eyes, and soothing power
Fill the sweet void of thy vacation hour!
But mark the lessons of my thoughtful lyre,
Think not, what pleases now, will never tire.

F I N I S.

www.ingramcontent.com/pod-product-compliance
Lightning Source LLC
Chambersburg PA
CBHW021458090426
42739CB00009B/1784

* 9 7 8 3 3 3 7 1 5 7 7 0 8 *